ADVA
THE FI
CO

MW00881708

"The Five Principles of Collaboration speaks on the very core of human existence......collaboration. Mr. Agbanyim brings this construct to life when he states "the optimistic act of working with one another encourages a life of gratitude." This book challenges traditional thinkers to critically examine their thought process on how to collaborate in the workplace, boardroom, marriage, academics, and other settings that involve human interactions. I recommend The Five Principles of Collaboration to corporate executives, managers, academic institutions, and anybody who likes to experience healthy human relationships."
—Frank Shankwitz, founder, Make-A-Wish Foundation

"No one exists on an island, and The Five Principles of Collaboration by J. Ibeh Agbanyim reminds us that our individual and personal successes always involve collaboration in one form or another. More specifically, this book looks at the power of collaboration through five concepts that, if fully understood, practiced, and promoted, can and will increase morale and any bottom line. Agbanyim's road map to collaboration includes everyday examples and a clear and accessible readability that is supported by careful industrial and scholarly research. This is surely a resource that many will read over and over to remind ourselves that we all have a

responsibility to each other to be our best selves in our workplace, in our homes, and in all of our relationships. There is certainly no success without collaboration."
—Neal A. Lester, PhD, Foundation Professor of English, Director of Project Humanities, Arizona State University

"'If you do not have faith in yourself, it will be difficult to trust others.' J. Ibeh Agbanyim's *The Five Principles of Collaboration* is a true guide to success not just in business but in the world. Anchored with the quote above, Agbanyim does an exceptional job of breaking down how to form powerful partnerships that both progress you forward and create lasting endeavors. As a CEO/Filmmaker in Hollywood, each chapter was essential to my career. Thus I immediately added this book to my intellectual tool box because having incredible collaboration skills is the root to our success. If you're having hardships keeping relationships, partners, friends, and so forth, start with this book and you will ultimately see a difference in your personal, future, and business lifestyle."
—Justin Chambers, Award-Winning Filmmaker, CEO Crevice Entertainment Company LLC, www.CreviceEntertainment.com

"What a pleasure reading, *The Five Principals of Collaboration,* which blends research and the art of vivid storytelling to bring to the forefront relevant issues such as bullying, respect, trust, and communication in the workplace and in our personal lives. Mr. Agbanyim provides straightforward ideas to develop and sustain healthier relationships through collaboration. The chapters on time management and effective communication are priceless—whether it is with our significant other, our children, family, friends, neighbors, co–workers, or boss. Mr. Agbanyim provides the tools to help us find solutions and take steps to build collaborative relationships and improve organizational productivity and personal bonds."

—Dr. Alberto M. Flores, Beyond the Vision, LLC

"Mr. J. Ibeh Agbanyim has made a wonderful contribution to relational psychology through the exploration of what it means to collaborate and co-exist peacefully in various facets of our lives. In this book, *The Five Principles of Collaboration,* he helps us to understand how to apply trust, respect, willingness, empowerment, and effective communication to human relationships. He walks us through the psychosocial dimensions in workplaces, homes, institutions, marital life, and how team/good rapport effect excellent raptorial efficacy in human relationship. This book makes for interesting reading. To enable the reader to learn the essential tools in applying the principles of collaboration, the author utilizes captivating relational stories to buttress his points. Thus, it goes without saying that this is a must-read book for all classes of people, especially those struggling with human relationships. I highly recommend it to all."

—Rev. Fidelis Igwenwanne, PhD, BCC, Chaplain, Mercy Gilbert Medical Center, Gilbert, AZ

THE FIVE PRINCIPLES

of

COLLABORATION

Applying Trust, Respect, Willingness, Empowerment, and Effective Communication to Human Relationships

J. IBEH AGBANYIM

THE FIVE PRINCIPLES OF COLLABORATION: APPLYING TRUST, RESPECT, WILLINGNESS, EMPOWERMENT, AND EFFECTIVE COMMUNICATION TO HUMAN RELATIONSHIPS

The information, ideas, and suggestions in this book are not intended as a substitute for professional advice. Before following any suggestions contained in this book, you should consult your personal physician or mental health professional. Neither the author nor the publisher shall be liable or responsible for any loss or damage allegedly arising as a consequence of your use or application of any information or suggestions in this book.

iUniverse books may be ordered through booksellers or by contacting:

iUniverse
1663 Liberty Drive
Bloomington, IN 47403
www.iuniverse.com
1-800-Authors (1-800-288-4677)

Because of the dynamic nature of the Internet, any web addresses or links contained in this book may have changed since publication and may no longer be valid. The views expressed in this work are solely those of the author and do not necessarily reflect the views of the publisher, and the publisher hereby disclaims any responsibility for them.

Any people depicted in stock imagery provided by Thinkstock are models, and such images are being used for illustrative purposes only.
Certain stock imagery © Thinkstock.

ISBN: 978-1-4917-6511-1 (sc)
ISBN: 978-1-4917-6512-8 (e)

Library of Congress Control Number: 2015906680

Print information available on the last page.

iUniverse rev. date: 07/01/2015

*To the universe because I believe
in the boomerang effect*

*What I put out in the universe is what comes
back to me. Therefore, I put out knowledge,
love, grace, new imagination, understanding,
forgiveness, and all the positive energies
that come from the writing of this book.*

CONTENTS

PREFACE

In my years of working in several industries (a semiconductor company, fast-food restaurants, entrepreneurial efforts, and distribution logistics), taking part in speaking engagements, writing books, and interacting with peers from all backgrounds in classrooms, one thing remains constant in all these relationships. Most people interact with one another based on preconceived notions about individuals and their groups, which find ways to express themselves through jokes, gestures, facial expressions, body postures, and eye-to-eye contact in several public spaces.

From personal experience, when I published my first book and discussed it with customers, acquaintances, and even strangers, all shared an initial question: "So you actually wrote this book by yourself?" This question puzzles me because it could mean several things:

1. I'm not capable enough to write a book.
2. Somebody must have written it for me.
3. I don't look like someone who could write anything worth reading.

When I hear people ask such a question, I normally pause and pleasantly stare at them, hoping they rephrase the question or further explain what they meant by it. It never fails. They always feel embarrassed and try to salvage the situation. But we pay deeper attention to how we express our memorized emotions toward a particular group, gender, ethnicity, national origin, religion, and so forth. And the same reaction applies in academic accomplishments.

I once attended a friend's graduation ceremony at a number-one ranked global MBA business university. During the procession, I was sitting next to a retired engineer who was attending his daughter's graduation ceremony. So as we tried to acquaint ourselves, I introduced myself, and he responded.

He next asked, "So what do you do for a living?"

I told him that I worked for X company as an industrial athlete, and he introduced himself as a retired engineer with a semi-conductor company. I noticed that his demeanor changed the moment I introduced myself as an industrial athlete. Immediately, he had already prejudged me based on my job description. But further into our discussion, he realized I had a graduate degree in industrial psychology and I was pursing my doctorate as well. All of a sudden, his demeanor became warm and pleasant toward me.

He had already prejudged me based on his limited knowledge about me as a person. Obviously, most people interact with others based on several layers and assumptions. But when those assumptions are biased, untested, and prejudicial in nature, it affects healthy relationships. I have based this book on how our hidden biases and unconscious behaviors toward one another can puncture relationships. If the principles of collaboration—trust, respect, willingness, empowerment, and effective communication—are positively channeled, they can energize relationships in the workplaces, social settings, and so forth.

As a person with a background in industrial psychology, authorship, speaking, and consulting, most people approach me through the lens of my expertise and do not generalize my existence. And I have noticed a significant shift in how these five principles play a major role in collaboration.

We build relationships around the concept of the five principles of collaboration. In other words, when any of these principles is lacking, human relationships suffer. Therefore, it is critical to understand these principles so relationships in workplace and social settings or on intrapersonal levels are healthy and engaging.

For example, in the workplace, healthy employee-management relationships exist when collaboration is present. In social settings, people create internal prison walls when collaboration is absent. Intrapersonal relationships are healthy when the "will to meaning"—humans' ability to understand their purpose in life and the way that purpose connects to other elements they encounter—is well established. Dr. Viktor Frankl rightly noted, "The most basic human motivation is the will to meaning."

Essentially, if the will to meaning is absent in any setting, anybody who encounters such a person will likely experience collaboration deficiency. Therefore, if we approach this concept of the five principles of collaboration with an open mind and curiosity, new information is contributed to the body of knowledge.

While there is no particular order of flow on how the five principles are expressed, I will shortly present a brief explanation to prepare readers with what to expect throughout the next few chapters. Importantly, I encourage readers to further their knowledge on these principles by further researching references that I have shared. The idea is that the more we know, the more we realize that we don't know.

That is, as we dig deeper in researching references discussed in this book, we realize that we are just scratching the surface. Therefore, I place great emphasis on encouraging readers to take notes and read more about the information I have provided in this book, as they will definitely expand their knowledge on the five principles of collaboration.

Studies show that 67 to 80 percent of second marriages end in divorce, while third marriages have an even higher rate of ending (Cepeda 2012). In other words, if couples fail to "stop the bleeding" in their first marriage by doing whatever it takes to rectify their differences, the same reasons why the first marriage failed are highly likely to resurface. Therefore, it is critical to examine the five principles of collaboration to sustain relationships at all levels.

Studies also show that loneliness in the workplace indicates distrust, suspicion, and fear, which invariably causes employees to avoid one another. In this context, trusting one another at the office is a recipe for a healthy work environment. Deep relationships that exist between people depend on the level of respect they have for each other.

When respect is lacking among friends, such relationships stand in limbo. Any effort to ignore or disregard the very fabric that sustains human relationships is lethal.

The level of willingness to collaborate determines the ability to engage in a conversation, perform in an event, demonstrate proficiency, or exhibit moral turpitude in any setting. In other words, the willingness to thrive in any endeavor creates relentless efforts and zealousness to collaborate with others. In the absence of willingness, collaborating with one another seems lackadaisical. I will examine an in-depth analysis to determine how the presence of willingness can enhance collaboration.

Empowerment also plays an integral role in a relationship. From behavioral and psychological dimensions, studies show that employee empowerment has proven to be a catalyst for job satisfaction. That is, when employees feel empowered, they will likely experience job satisfaction. I can explain empowerment as when an individual in a position of advantage shares his or her knowledge and data with subordinates. Such exercise increases motivation, trust, communication, and a whole host of other constructs. For example, when people in a relationship feel empowered, it flourishes the bond, if well directed.

Effective communication opens the door into understanding and action. An effective communicator can use descriptive words to bring response into a situation. To measure the impact of how an effective communicator interacts with another person, watch the receiver's body language and gestures. A skillful communicator pays attention to words and listens diligently. Listening is an art, as it enhances clarity and engagement. Therefore, an effective communicator possesses all these components so he or she can promote collaboration.

You cannot achieve the principles listed in this book without diligence, an act of discipline. Studies show that dental students' diligence is a statistically significant predictor of their academic performance (Arthur, Shepherd, and Sumo 2006). Evidently, doing the same thing repeatedly eventually brings a significant and measurable result. Therefore, diligence is required to realize a measurable result in the area of collaboration.

Time is a precious gift to all living creatures. Every living organism came to existence with time. It brought great people into discoveries. One of the best pieces of music ever produced was produced in and with time. We remember historical moments in life with time. How we utilize our hours, minutes, and seconds determines how accomplished (spiritually, emotionally, economically, relationally, and so forth) we become.

Time is a double-edged sword! It can elevate one

to greatness when it is utilized judiciously, or it can destroy minds when misused and abused. The Wendelien (2003) study on time management concluded that time management training is helpful in reducing worry and procrastination at work. Based on the researcher's conclusion, the ability to manage time judiciously significantly reduces worry or unhealthy stress.

In substance, if managing our time helps reduce unwarranted stresses, it is enough reason to pay particular attention to managing how we spend our hours. In practice, studies show that the average American watches five hours of TV per day. Comparatively, African Americans watch an average of 218 hours of television a month, whites watch 155.3 hours, Hispanics watch an average of 123.2 hours, and Asian Americans watch an average of 92.3 hours (Hinckley 2014). The less TV we watch, the more time we have to think, engage, network, contribute, and so forth with ourselves and others. Therefore, time wisely utilized translates into self-improvement and a measurable result.

This book challenges you to ask yourself, *Am I diligent in applying these five principles? Am I eager to challenge my old way of thinking? Am I willing to entertain new imagination?* This book will guide you in answering these questions.

REFERENCES

Agbanyim, J. I. *The Power of Engagement: How to Find Balance in Work and Life.* Bloomington, Ind.: iUniverse, 2012.

Arthur, C., L. Shepherd, and M. Sumo. "The Role of Students' Diligence in Predicting Academic Performance." *Research in the Schools* 13, no. 2 (2006): 72–80. http://search.proquest.com/docview/211054372?accountid=35812.

Cepeda, M. "Shine: 7 Divorce Myths—Debunked!" http://shine.yahoo.com/love-sex/7-divorce-myths-8212-debunked-170300654.html.

Frankl, V. E. *Man's Search for Meaning.* Boston, Mass.: Beacon Press, 2006.

Hinckley, D. "Average American Watches 5 Hours of TV Per Day, Report Shows." Accessed February 23, 2015. http://www.nydailynews.com/life-style/average-american-watches-5-hours-tv-day-article-1.1711954.

Korkki, P. "Workstation: Building a Bridge to a Lonely Colleague." Accessed July 5, 2014. http://www.nytimes.com/2012/01/29/jobs/building-a-bridge-to-a-lonelycolleague-workstation.html?_r=1&src=tp.

Pelit, E., Yüksel Öztürk, and Yalçin Arslantürk. "The Effects of Employee Empowerment on Employee Job Satisfaction." *International Journal of Contemporary Hospitality Management* 23, no. 6 (2011): 784–802. doi: http://dx.doi.org/10.1108/09596111111153475.

Wendelien, V. E. (2003). Procrastination at Work and Time Management Training. *The Journal of Psychology* 137 (5)(2003): 421–34. http://search.proquest.com/docview/213832328?accountid=35812.

ACKNOWLEDGMENTS

I am grateful to God, who has given me the opportunity to meet great men and women of this generation and ability to put thoughts and imagination in print. And I treasure my relationship with him.

It has been a fun experience to write this book. As always, thought and experience precedes every action. The idea of making a book out of the topic started with my first book, *The Power of Engagement*. While I enjoyed writing my first book, I found particular delight in presenting *The Five Principles of Collaboration* as a subchapter of chapter 7 (Leading by Example) of the book.

Another surprise surfaced when I presented the five principles of collaboration as a subtopic at the University of Ibadan during a multidisciplinary seminar series in 2013. It was well received by an audience of master's and doctoral students under the directions of Dr. Aleremi Alarape, Sub Dean (Arts and Humanities) at Postgraduate School, University of Ibadan.

At a 2014 ASQ Technical Communities Conference in Orlando, the audience also very highly rated my presentation on the topic. Fast-forward to 2015: when the manuscript was 60 percent completed, I shared it with my friend, Alberto Flores, PhD, and he expressed great interest and suggested I write my dissertation on the topic, but I decided to go ahead and publish it instead. I will write a second edition in the near future. Obviously, the content was intriguing and relevant. When I decided to turn it into a book, I knew it was the right thing to do.

My appreciation goes to Dr. Aleremi Alarape, who believed in my work and invited me to share it at the Department of Psychology 2013 seminar. It meant a lot to those students who participated and me. My colleague Adil Dalal invited me to present the topic at the American Society for Quality conference in Florida. Alberto Flores showed interest in the topic and encouraged me to proceed in the publication.

As we live in this world of learning, we never know how much powerful, constructive ideas are worth until we share them with people.

I find delight in reading Jim Stovall's book *The Millionaire Map*. It is an asset because Mr. Stovall strongly believes that "you change your life when you change your mind, and you have the right to choose, and you are one quality decision away from anything you want." The entire book contains nuggets of wisdom.

When I met Mr. Stovall at Klemmer & Associates Leadership Development Training in San Diego, his speaking engagement to business leaders from all over the globe was a testament to his intellectual humility.

And I was compelled to read more of his books, which have been an agent of change for me. We have remained friends ever since, and I treasure his friendship.

To my lovely wife and beautiful daughter, I appreciate your contributions into my life, and I share my world with you too.

INTRODUCTION

Duffy (2014) argued that the best ideas are always the product of collaboration. By implication, collaboration is an essential element in producing practical ideas. It is difficult to create, invent, or produce quality ideas or products without collaborative exercise. Duffy (2014) further suggested that collaboration is a mutual intervention and progressive interaction with objects of discourse.

Baird and Wang (2010) pointed out that one of the four different dimensions of employee empowerment is collaboration. That is, in a collaborative work environment, employees feel empowered and have measurable sense of direction.

So collaboration evidently contributes to employee empowerment. Based on researchers' conclusions in their studies, employee empowerment has a background in collaboration. Therefore, empowered employees are likely to work together.

A recent study conducted by researchers Haun, Rekers, and Tomasello, published in *Association for Psychological Science Journal*, concluded that social learning differs between humans and nonhumans. Humans are more readily able to conform socially than great apes are. All primates learn conspecific things socially, but it is unclear whether they conform to the behavior of these conspecifics (Haun et al. 2014). Evidently, humans become what they expose themselves to. That is, we become who we socialize with.

If evidence is clear in this case, people should take it more seriously whom they allow in their space. Collaborating with the wrong crowd could very much produce the wrong actions. In the context of applying the five principles of collaboration and the ways they strengthen human relationships, associating with the wrong crowd could distort how clearly these principles are applied. Therefore, there are good reasons to adhere to these principles.

It is also critical to understand that unnecessary conformities could distort good intentions. So for an optimized result, even in the workplace, people should be selective in their social endeavors. Associating with employees who will motivate and engage in activities that produce desired results is important.

The premise of science and experience led me to believe that, if people are presented with the right tools (environment, equipment, ideas, and involvement), the five principles of collaboration as shared in this text (respect, trust, willingness, empowerment, and effective communication) will likely bring out the best in people, be it in the workplace, social settings, or relationships. It has also been tested individually that all these constructs can play a major role in collaboration; however, it is unclear how, when combined, they could improve human interactions with one another.

Viewing these constructs as individual and bringing them together is an adventure worth exploring. This book's premise is to challenge readers to look into each one of these constructs and determine which are more prevalent in their lives and which guide them to live lives of impact as they relate to collaboration and relationships.

From a scholarly and experiential standpoint, Congress passed the Violent Crime Control and Law Enforcement Act twenty years ago and laid the groundwork for establishing community policing as the national paradigm in order to build partnerships between police officers and the residents they serve, a collaborative problem-solving approach.

The intent of the approach was to introduce ways to shift police officers from the mind-set of using forces to control crime to finding collaborative measures to improve quality of life (Clay 2015). *Monitor on Psychology,* a publication of the American Psychological Association, is in the forefront, advocating to build trust between police officers and the communities they are policing.

In this context, when distrust and a lack of willingness to change is present, it will be difficult to achieve such a goal. Evidently, there is a strong relationship between trust, willingness, and collaboration. Tom R. Tyler, PhD, noted, "There's very clear research to suggest that when police undermine trust, they promote crime" (Clay 2015). Clearly, trust is a pivotal element for fighting crime. That is, crime will likely drop when trust is upheld to a high standard between police officers and the residents of communities they serve.

REFERENCES

Baird, K., and H. Wang. "Employee Empowerment: Extent of Adoption and Influential Factors." *Personnel Review* 39, no. 5 (2010): 574–599. doi: http://dx.doi.org/10.1108/00483481011064154.

Clay, A. "Post-Ferguson: An APA-Sponsored Briefing on Capitol Hill Showcased the Role Psychologists Can Play in Building Trust between Police and Community." *APA Monitor on Psychology* 46, no. 1 (February 2015): 16.

Duffy, W. "Collaboration (in) Theory: Reworking the Social Turn's Conversational Imperative." *College English* 76, no. 5 (2014): 416–435. http://search.proquest.com/docview/1518535076?accountid=35812.

Haun, B. M., Y. Rekers, and M. Tomasello. "Children Conform to the Behavior of Peers: Other Great Apes Stick with What They Know." *Psychological Science: Research, Theory, & Application in Psychology and Related Sciences* 25, no. 12 (February 2015): 2,160.

CHAPTER 1

TRUST

Trust is a critical element in all facets of human relationships, whether in business, marriage, friendship, academic institutions, or communities. Trust enhances relationships; lack of it destroys relationships.

Racial tension existing in Ferguson, Missouri, explains the deep divide between African Americans and the Ferguson Police Department. The underlying divide is a lack of trust on the part of the police department. A recently concluded investigation conducted by the US Department of Justice (USDOJ) outlined evidence that validated why racial tension exists in Ferguson (United States Department of Justice 2015). While details of the investigation is not this chapter's intent, it is critical to note how damaging distrust can be to communities, organizations, groups, and on individual levels.

From a psychological standpoint, it is difficult to collaborate with individuals, communities, or organizations when trust is lacking. An absence of trust can cause misjudgment, exaggeration, untested assumptions, micromanagement, and so forth. That is why it is important to understand a situation in its entirety before disagreeing.

While addressing law students at Oklahoma City University, Supreme Justice Sonia Sotomayor made a profound statement that I deemed fit to share in my work. She was advising the law students to learn how to listen with their whole being during cross-examination in court. She was implying that an effective attorney ought to listen and establish eye-to-eye contact with the subject during cross-examination.

Cross-examination is not the time to take notes. Rather, it is the time to listen actively because body language, gestures, and other nonverbal communications are the most powerful indicators of understanding an individual. And it is difficult to understand someone when distracted. And when preoccupied, it is easy to start disagreeing without understanding the entire case.

In her own words, she said, "Hearing is not the same as agreeing. You can hear things and disagree, but you are not entitled to disagree until you understand" (VanTimmeren 2014).

It is difficult to apply what Justice Sotomayor said if we lack trust in ourselves. Having faith in oneself is a critical component for discipline and vulnerability. And understanding oneself makes a world of difference on how we view the world and our environment. So trusting oneself is a critical element in collaboration.

For example, if you do not have faith in yourself, it will be difficult to trust others. It would be challenging to have confidence in someone else to the point of collaborating with him or her. So I pose this question to you, *Do you trust yourself? Do you know who you are and what your capabilities are?*

Throughout this book, we will stay on this track of knowing who we are as individuals and not as a group. When these questions are not satisfactorily answered, it is difficult to work together with people. In terms of viewing trust as a collaborative mechanism, one has to know his or her limitations and capabilities before trusting someone else. Because of a lack of trust, relationships collapse, and organizations go out of business because the CEO does not have confidence in his or her frontline employees. Studies show that trust overshadows loneliness in the workplace.

For example, for employees who feel distrust from their management and colleagues, such sentiment provokes a negative view about the company. And when an ill perspective is hovering around the workplace, negative energy and distrust infects such atmosphere. Coworkers and management can fill an office, yet a person will feel very lonely because trust is the missing ingredient.

Darabi and Clark (2012) noted that trust in individuals is fundamental to collaborative settings from both practitioner and academic points of view. Therefore, trust is an integral part of working together. Collaboration may cease to exist in the absence of trust. From the researchers' perspective, networking is a key ingredient to creating initial trust (Darabi and Clark 2012).

In this context, collaboration is built around networking and initiating trust. It is reasonable to imply that trust and collaboration work hand in hand. When trust is distorted, the process of working together becomes hindered. Recent studies on gender differences and trust argued that female workers are likely to take jobs with higher values of trust but lower income than men (Helliwell and Huang 2011). In this context, business leaders who understand this statement could create a collaborative work environment that reflects their value of trust.

Let's visit the different types of trust that exist in human relationships: contractual trust, competence trust, and goodwill trust. Each level determines how far collaborations or relationships will go. We will explain each construct in a way that makes sense, so when we claim that we do not trust somebody, we can ask ourselves, "At what level am I not trusting him or her?"

Understanding these levels of trusts will help us decide at what level to trust a person and why we should not dismiss people simply because they violate one type of trust and not all three. It is possible not to trust somebody on one level and yet trust him or her on another. Unfortunately, we habitually dismiss people based on an overarching claim of trust, as opposed to examining trust in its entirety.

Contractual Trust

Contractual trust refers to basic trust, and it can be verbal or written. For example, you and a friend have agreed to meet for lunch at a Houston restaurant by noon. Come noon, your friend is nowhere to be found, and he shows up at one thirty without having called you. This friend has violated your contractual trust because he never made an effort to call or text you that he would be running late. Interestingly, he habitually shows up late to appointments with you. In this context, such person has an issue of keeping to time, so he cannot be trusted in that aspect of his life.

In another example, you and a skilled plumber entered into a written contract for him to do work for you. He asked for 20 percent down to start the work, and you paid him the amount. He showed up on time but worked halfway and decided to come back after lunch to finish the work. After lunch, he never returned. In this context, he has violated your contractual trust for not completing the job.

In considering these two scenarios, the skilled plumber showed up on time but could not complete the job. Evidently, he was on time but unreliable in finishing his work. Is it possible that he shows up on time for the social aspect of his life (e.g., a Super Bowl game) but arrives late to work-related meetings?

It is reasonable to conclude that he is reliable in social functions but unreliable when it is related to work. After making these distinctions, you can decide whether to keep him as a social friend and not as a business acquaintance. So you could trust him from a social standpoint but not a business position.

Contractual trust exists in a collaborative atmosphere. For functional collaboration to take place, people need to understand each other at that level, knowing that the relationship exists within the parameter of contractual trust. In other words, a relationship between two people exists expressly because they maintain verbal or written contractual trusts. When that happens, it is easy to collaborate with one another on a contractual trust level. Research shows that a healthy contractual trust reduces transactional cost, increases sociability, and serves as the basis for cooperation.

For example, collaboration based on contractual trust can warrant a business owner to offer a discount or even credit to his or her client. Both parties feel comfortable around each other, which creates a sociable atmosphere on both a business and social level, simply as a result of collaborating on a contractual level of trust.

Contractual trust and competence types of trust are intertwined, except that competence trust is based on skills, knowledge, and trainings. Competence trust requires skillful trainings and a higher level of responsibility, and it can be a distinction between life and death. Competence trust is essential for a person of authority in his or her field of discipline.

Competence Trust

Competence trust comes with skills, knowledge, or experience about a particular area or trade. A person who operates on a competence trust has a skill or profession (engineering, medicine, psychology, athletic ability, piloting, etc.) that distinguishes him or her from everybody else in a crowd. So when someone has confidence in you on a competence level, it means you have a skill worth trusting for. Based on that skill, one can decide to hire you for an assignment or project.

For example, most pregnant women give birth to their children in hospitals where trained nurses and doctors are available to practice delivery routines. So when pregnant women head to the hospital to give birth, they trust the delivery crew on a competence level. That is, they trust that the applications that nurses and doctors will administer for delivery of their babies are practiced enough to be trusted.

In this context, is it possible that the same medical practitioners could not be dependable in a social setting? Meaning that on the level of their expertise, they are trusted but not on the social level of trust. It is important to understand that we can trust people on different levels without assuming that, if they disappoint you on contractual level, they could let you down on a competence level as well. Your assumptions may be inconclusive.

People who are trusted on a competence level have proven proficiency and high professional standards.

They are also trusted enough to honestly convey information. That is, when competence trust exists in a relationship, information flows freely without any distrust or untested assumptions. And when trust is mutual, collaboration is present.

For example, patients go to doctors based on competence trust. Patients may not necessarily have to know their doctors on a personal level. Rather, they know them in a competence arena. Patients also trust their doctors not to share their medical information with people without their approval in writing. When we can define the type of trust we have in our doctors, then it is easy to collaborate with them on a competence level. Patient/doctor confidentiality expressly and legally depends on competence trust. When this competence trust is violated, the parties involved are hurt, and this can cause permanent damage in relationships and, in extreme cases, a lawsuit.

A pop star died as a result of a doctor's negligence in administering propofol, a powerful sedative that only practitioners within the operating room world use (Kotler 2010), a clear example of abuse of competence trust. The patient trusted his doctor to administer the right dosage that would allow him to sleep, but the practitioner negligently left him to die. Competence trust is lethal if misused and could cause death in a matter of seconds.

Having known what you know about contractual and competence types of trust, another type of trust is more common than you imagine, goodwill trust.

Goodwill Trust

Goodwill trust is based on mutual expectations of open commitment to each other (Green 2003). This type of trust suggests that, at a glance, people ought to give each other a certain God-given trust just for being human beings. In other words, it is reasonable when we see another person to trust him or her on a goodwill level, having faith that we can at least greet each other as human beings before getting to know one another on deeper levels.

Goodwill trust also posits that we have good intentions for one another until behavior starts to shift either through deeper conversations or acts. This type of trust transcends race, culture, gender, and age. For example, when we meet someone for the first time in an elevator, the human thing to do is to be cordial to each other for that period of time, simply because we possess human features.

For example, if you see an eight-hundred-pound lion inside the elevator after the door opened, the human thing to do is to flee because a lion is wild and dangerous and does not possess human features. However, if you meet another human being in an elevator, your first instinct is hopefully to be friendly because you share human features with that person. It is humanistic to behave that way.

Another way to view goodwill trust is from an aspect of social and corporate responsibilities. For example, we give back to a community that we invest in.

In our neighborhood subdivisions, it is humanistic to ensure that we look out for each other simply because we share neighborhoods and want our children to live in a safe and healthy environment. From this standpoint, we share goodwill trust by looking out for each other on that level without getting into spying or stalking each other. We demonstrate goodwill trust when we share this simple concept. It is an unwritten way of life to assume a safe and healthy environment for your neighbors until certain circumstances create separations or suspicions.

From corporate social responsibility perspectives, goodwill trust suggests that organizations should invest back in the community they operate businesses in. That is why some companies open charitable activities and environmental stewardship (Pimple 2012). Some American multinational organizations have their employees volunteer to give back to the communities (e.g., donating employee time for going to food banks and serving the less privileged or sharing writing materials with struggling neighborhoods). Some churches do missionary work outside the country, building houses for the poor. Hospitals provide medical treatment to abandoned communities. And so forth and so forth.

Goodwill trust in this context means that communities expect companies to reinvest in the populations they serve to improve the residents' quality of life. So trust is evidently a collaborative exercise. No one can claim monopoly on collaboration without trusting another person to engage. And when goodwill trust flourishes, it creates a critical success factor. There are so many benefits in applying trust as a collaborative mechanism, especially in the workplace:

- Trust increases life satisfaction over income.
- Female workers are likely to take jobs with higher values of trust but lower income than men (Helliwell and Huang 2011).
- Trust increases employee well-being.
- Trust creates mutual expectations.
- Trust is a skill that needs to be learned.

Trust as a construct is a secret ingredient of life. When individuals, families, communities, and organizations operate on the wheels of trust, human relationships are improved. Therefore, share this text with your loved ones and have a conversation at a dinner table on how to improve well-being from a position of trust. Ask yourself:

- How satisfied can I be if I take a dose of trust on a daily basis?
- If I had sixty seconds to live, what would I do differently to trust people based on these three levels?

The next chapter addresses respect as a mechanism for collaboration. That is, how healthy are relationships without the presence of respect? Can we view respect differently from professional perspectives? Does respect have a stake on structural empowerment? We attempt to answer some of these questions in this chapter. Hopefully, we will gain knowledge from examining respect from these scopes.

REFERENCES

Darabi, F., and M. Clark. "Developing Business School/SMEs Collaboration: The Role of Trust." *International Journal of Entrepreneurial Behaviour & Research* 18, no. 4 (2012): 477–493. doi: http://dx.doi.org/10.1108/13552551211239500.

Green, R. "Measuring Goodwill Trust between Groups of People: Three Years of an Oil Industry Alliance." *Strategic Change* 12, no. 7 (2003): 367–379. http://search.proquest.com/docview/216508600?accountid=35812.

Helliwell, J. F., and H. Huang. "Well-Being and Trust in the Workplace." *Journal of Happiness Studies* 12, no. 5 (2011): 747–767. doi: http://dx.doi.org/10.1007/s10902-010-9225-7.

Ibrahim, M., and P. M. Ribbers. "The Impacts of Competence-Trust and Openness-Trust on Interorganizational Systems." *European Journal of Information Systems* 18, no. 3 (2009): 223–234. doi: http://dx.doi.org/10.1057/ejis.2009.17.

Kotler, R. "Secrets of a Beverly Hills Cosmetic Surgeon." http://blogs.webmd.com/cosmetic-surgery/2010/02/michael-jacksons-doctor-indicted.html.

Korkki, P. "Workstation: Building a Bridge to a Lonely Colleague." Accessed July 5, 2014. http://www.nytimes.com/2012/01/29/jobs/building-a-bridge-to-a-lonelycolleague-workstation.html?_r=1&src=tp.

McGrath, C., and D. M. Zell. "Profiles of Trust: Who to Turn to and For What." *MIT Sloan Management Review* 50, no. 2 (2009): 75–80. http://search.proquest.com/docview/224966770?accountid=35812.

Pimple, M. M. "Business Ethics and Corporate Social Responsibility." *International Journal of Management Research and Reviews* 2, no. 5 (2012): 761–765. http://search.proquest.com/docview/1425249063?accountid=35812.

United States Department of Justice. "Investigation of Ferguson Police Department, United States Department of Justice Civil Rights Division." Accessed March 4, 2015. http://www.justice.gov/sites/default/files/opa/press-releases/attachments/2015/03/04/ferguson_police_department_report.pdf.

VanTimmeren, C. "U.S. Supreme Court Justice Sonia Sotomayor visits OKC." http://www.okcfox.com/story/26513632/us-supreme-court-justice-sonia-sotomayor-visits-okc.

CHAPTER 2

RESPECT

High school students Dale and Derrick get into a verbal fight as to who is the smartest kid in class. While Dale is attempting to brag using hand gestures to express his feelings, Derrick takes offense and yells at Dale. Shortly after, Dale's cousin gets involved, and a fight breaks out.

Mrs. Houston, a PE teacher with twenty years of experience in the school, overheard Dale using vulgarity at Derrick, and she raised her voice to defend Derrick. When word got to the school superintendent, both Dale's and Derrick's parents heard what happened, and they were frustrated. Unfortunately, Mrs. Houston was fired for shouting at Dale. Other teachers were shocked when they heard she was let go.

If you had an opportunity to talk to the school authority, what would be your response to the situation? We know this about Mrs. Houston.

1.   She taught at her school for over twenty years.

2. Both students and fellow teachers liked her.
3. She had a good work history.

There is no right or wrong answer, so how do you feel about the school's reaction toward the teacher? Do you think the school did the right thing by firing her, or do you think they overreacted? Did she deserve to be let go considering her academic history?

Whatever answer you give is good enough. This analogy might sound too pedestrian, but it is a true story. I have withheld the actual names and location for obvious reasons.

Restorative justice is a growing movement to promote collaboration in educational, criminal justice, and other settings where people interact (DeAngelis 2014). Psychologists and criminal justice systems are using this approach to force law-breaking individuals to make amends with the community, as opposed to giving them heavier punishments. Studies show that the application of restorative justice reduced school suspensions at Cole Middle School in Oakland, California, by 89 percent and reduced the suspension rate at Richmond High School in Richmond, California, by 50 percent (DeAngelis 2014).

The idea is to allow the perpetrator and victim to talk about their issues face-to-face in a safe atmosphere and discuss how the perpetrator's behavior affected the victim. Once this discussion and assignment are met and resolved, the group accepts the person back into its midst.

This approach is very practical and relevant in several ways. First, it allows parties involved in the argument to have an opportunity to look into each other's eyes and discuss issues at hand. By hopefully creating a safe environment for such discussion, it will encourage human-to-human relationships for the sharing of similarities rather than differences within one another. Second, it teaches us how to problem solve and collaborate in difficult situations. Third, it promotes respect and peace in relationships.

1. Respect has a boomerang effect. It's a two-way street. We give respect to receive it. It's difficult to give respect to a person who has no regard for you. In other words, respect cannot exist in an atmosphere of pretense. For example, people may say they have respect for their abusive bosses, but is it really respect or just pretense? Studies show that structural empowerment has a direct effect on respect and organizational trust (Laschinger et al. 2005).

2. This seems to suggest that respect is an intentional act. It's a deliberate and conscious act, not a random one. Respect requires some processes and exists person to person, community to community, organization to organization, and nation to nation. Therefore, to respect a person, community, or nation requires having a structure in place. Respect is based on

experience about the person or a group memory about a particular person's contributions.

3. Respect is also based on history. For example, people and organizations give particular respect to graduates of Harvard, Yale, Princeton, Columbia, and other Ivy League universities, an evidence of reputation. Because of this, we expect graduates from these universities to act in a certain way. Organizations that hire individuals from these universities collaborate effectively with those graduates based on respect and high expectations. Therefore, it is reasonable to note that respect is earned and not given.

4. In a collaborative environment, people respect each other so they can experience maximum results. An environment of respect shapes social engagement and well-being (Huo et al. 2010). That is, a social environment where respect of one another prevails promotes social engagement and well-being. People tend to be engaged and have healthier outlooks on their lives. Evidently, when an environment lacks people who respect one another, social engagement and well-being are affected as well. Based on these observations and reports, it is critical to understand that a lack of respect directly impacts how people collaborate, and it affects their health.

One study (Beach et al. 2007) shows that there is a profoundly different outcome based on the way that doctors perceive their patients. It can be tempting for a doctor to view his or her patient as an ill person and treat him or her based on that label as a "patient," ignoring the fact that the patient is also a person. Such a perception can impact how doctors treat their patients. This study revealed that, when doctors perceive patients as sick (cognitive dimension) but not as people (behavioral dimension), they create an atmosphere of disrespect. Conversely, when an individual is viewed as both a patient and a person, mutual respect is established.

In the context of researchers' views about respect, their approach has both a cognitive (believing that patients have values) and behavioral (acting in accordance with this belief) dimension.

Is it possible that, in other situations, we also view people based on their circumstances and not the quality of relationships? The above study seems to imply that we can easily label people for what they're struggling with and not who they are.

As in the case of the doctor-and-patient relationship, it is important that we always acknowledge each other's cognitive and behavioral dimensions, which means believing that patients have values and act in accordance with this belief (Beach et al. 2007). The study also highlights the importance of respecting patients' cultural differences as well. Acknowledging these dissimilarities speaks on the importance of respecting one another.

Factors Defining Disrespect in Relationships

Incivility is one cause of disrespect in a relationship. What is considered workplace incivility, as Andersson and Pearson described in their 1999 study, is any low-intensity deviant behavior with ambiguous intent to harm the target in violation of workplace norms for mutual respect (Cortina et al. 2001). So whenever an employee, supervisor, or manager looks at another person in a condescending manner, such behavior is considered workplace incivility.

For instance, some managers have formed a habit of writing reports on their computers and avoiding eye contact while an employee is reporting his or her concerns to them. This is evidently workplace incivility. Of about 1,180 public-sector employees surveyed in the past five years, 71 percent of them reported experiencing workplace incivility.

It is important to be self-aware of these microaggressive and psychological aggressive behaviors and avoid exhibiting them to other people. By implication, in an environment where people feel workplace incivility, they will experience issues with collaboration. When people feel that their presence is not important or relevant, such feeling hinders the act of working together. Lack of interest, disengagement, aloofness, job dissatisfaction, and a host of other negative emotions are results of disrespect in relationships, whether in work, social, or other setting.

Bullying also defines disrespect in the workplace. It is far more common than we think. One study defines bullying as repeated actions and practices of an unwanted nature that are directed against one or more employees. It is possible that some people exhibit this behavior either deliberately or unconsciously. However exercised, it can cause offense, distress, and humiliation (McKay et al. 2008). Evidence shows that humiliation is a traumatic state of mind and a ticking bomb for violence (Trumbull 2008). When employees feel bullied or humiliated, not only after working overtime, it can cause health concerns and result in employee turnover.

Bullying as a construct is a real threat to health. In the workplace, managers who use bullying or humiliation as tactics to motivate employees are indirectly and dangerously contributing to health issues of their employees. Taylor, Repetti, and Seeman (1997) shared in their study that an unhealthy environment is that which threatens safety and is conflictual, abusive, or violent in nature.

For example, when employees find it difficult to relate to their manager due to his or her behavior toward workers, such an environment is unhealthy because workers will withhold information out of destructive fear of retaliation or unfair treatment from management. A suppressed emotion causes stress, and chronic stress or unexpressed emotion threatens health. Therefore, a person in a position of authority should be aware of these red flags and make a conscious effort to treat work environment with an attitude to promote a healthy and respectable atmosphere.

The next chapter discusses the importance of the willingness to collaborate. Willingness to collaborate with others requires conscious effort and self-awareness.

REFERENCES

Beach, M. C., P. S. Duggan, C. K. Cassel, and G. Geller, G. "What Does 'Respect' Mean? Exploring the Moral Obligation of Health Professionals to Respect Patients." *Journal of General Internal Medicine* 22, no. 5 (2007): 692–5. doi: http://dx.doi.org/10.1007/s11606-006-0054-7.

Cortina, L. M., V. J. Magley, J. H. Williams, and R. D. Langhout. "Incivility in the Workplace: Incidence and Impact. *Journal of Occupational Health Psychology* 6, no. 1 (2001): 64–80. doi: http://dx.doi.org/10.1037/1076-8998.6.1.64.

DeAngelis, T. "Building Resilience among Black Boys." *Monitor on Psychology* 45, no. 9 (October 2014): 53.

Huo, Y. J., L. E. Molina, K. R. Binning, and S. P. Funge. "Subgroup Respect, Social Engagement, and Well-Being: A Field Study of an Ethnically Diverse High School." *Cultural Diversity and Ethnic Minority Psychology* 16, no. 3 (2010): 427–436. doi: http://dx.doi.org/10.1037/a0019886.

Mckay, R., D. H. Arnold, J. Fratzl, and R. Thomas. "Workplace Bullying in Academia: A Canadian Study." *Employee Responsibilities and Rights Journal* 20, no. 2 (2008): 77–100. doi: http://dx.doi.org/10.1007/s10672-008-9073-3.

Spence Laschinger, H. K., and J. Finegan. "Using Empowerment to Build Trust and Respect in the Workplace: A Strategy for Addressing the Nursing Shortage." *Nursing Economics* 23, no. 1 (2005): 6–13, 3. http://search.proquest.com/docview/236934609?accountid=35812.

Taylor, S. E., R. L. Repetti, and T. Seeman. "Health Psychology: What Is an Unhealthy Environment and How Does It Get Under the Skin?" *Annual Review of Psychology* 48 (1997): 411–47. http://search.proquest.com/docview/205799464?accountid=35812.

Trumbull, D. "Humiliation: The Trauma of Disrespect." *Journal of the American Academy of Psychoanalysis and Dynamic Psychiatry* 36, no. 4 (2008): 643–60. http://search.proquest.com/docview/198202294?accountid=35812.

CHAPTER 3

WILLINGNESS

The willingness to collaborate with one another is a critical element in relationships. A mother and daughter get along in mutual fashion when both have the desire to participate. Father-and-son relationships suffer when either or both lack the willingness to collaborate with one another. Employee-and-employer relationships thrive when the willingness to work together exists. Communities team up to fight neighborhood crimes when they share a common theme. Nations rise against others when none is willing to yield for peaceful negotiations. A couple divorces each other when the willingness to work on the relationship is dampened. A student fails an exam the moment he or she stops caring about making good grades. Church members stop attending services when interests and expectations start to sway.

The list goes on how a simple shift in thought process can change the course of action or relationship between two parties. Willingness speaks on the very core of contributing for a cause. In other words, the moment there's a desire to participate for whatever reason, an act of willingness has been activated. That is why it is critical to pay attention to those micro behaviors that exist whenever people are engaged in activities. The "dance" takes place whenever people are involved in any kind of experience, which speaks volumes about the mind-set of people involved and how willing they are in the process.

It is difficult to work with one another when the zeal is not present. One study suggested that willingness to sacrifice in close relationships was associated with strong commitment, high satisfaction, poor alternatives, and high investment (Van Lange et al. 1997).

In this context, when one is committed and satisfied and has no alternatives at the moment and a vested interest, such person is acting out of willingness, whether in a work, social, or any other relationship that involves more than one person. On the other hand, when these factors listed as evidence of willingness are missing, then the willingness to sacrifice is missed as well.

Let's use an analogy to demonstrate willingness to sacrifice.

"PLAYING HOOKY"

"Playing hooky," an American term, describes when a person decides to skip school, work, or other personal activity without an excuse, usually to take care of personal needs, regroup from stressful workweek, or do something exciting.

For example, an employee at a security company had worked sixty-five hours each workweek for months at a time. His long work hours had started to affect how attentive he was in making sure the company building was safe.

After a Saturday workday, he mentioned to his supervisor about taking off Monday to regroup, but his manager downplayed his request and turned deaf to his demand. Come Monday, the employee did not show up for work.

When his supervisor called his house, the employee told him that he had overslept due to fatigue and burnout. In the end, the employee never showed for work, and his supervisor could not discipline him for obvious reasons because he told his supervisor ahead of time and expected his supervisor to listen and respect his burnout concerns.

Based on information provided (i.e., sixty-five hours per week for months at a time), the employee was overworked and ignored when he finally requested a day off. His supervisor ignoring his request discouraged the employee from showing up for work. Clearly, he was not willing to work that day because he wanted to stay home and play hooky.

Evidently, when willingness is lacking in any experience, collaboration is likely to suffer. That is, the desire to collaborate with a boss, partner, spouse, colleague, and so forth is threatened when the willingness to work together is lacking. Some factors influence willingness and encourage a person to make a conscious decision on whether to collaborate or not.

GREATER AWARENESS

When a person is aware of the benefits or consequences associated with a decision, he or she is likely to engage willingly either to do it or not. In a case of an employee with a drug abuse issue who becomes aware of an Employee Assistance Program (EAP) his company is offering to employees with similar issues, he is likely to engage in such program willingly (Reynolds and Lehman 2003).

That is, greater awareness to a particular situation provokes the willingness to engage in finding solutions to that specific event. And when willingness is present in a particular experience, collaboration takes place. This is enough reason to pay attention to what we are (or are not) willing to do because results are based on our levels of collaboration.

For example, if we are less aware of a particular situation, the willingness to collaborate is minimal. But when full awareness is present, collaboration is maximized, which seems to suggest that adequate information is critical in decision making. And the ability and humility to identify valuable information when presented is paramount.

HUMILITY INVOLVES SELF-REGULATION

An article published in *Harvard Business Review* in 2014 emphasized that the best leaders are the humble ones, which seems to suggest that humility is a virtue or way of life.

It is a virtue because humble leaders speak in few words and demonstrate their intentions with ease and grace, as opposed to rage and arrogance. The article further explains that humble leaders are easily accessible in a diverse group. For a good leader to be able to relate with employees from different groups, humility is one quality such leader should possess. People who are from different persuasions than their boss are attracted to leaders who make them feel included in their work team, and it is true for both men and women. Humility can be attracting and engaging.

The former GE CEO, Jack Welch, once said that a good leader engages his or her employees by letting them understand the reason why they're there and leading them to believe in the purpose and to buy into it with their hearts and souls as well as their minds. A leader is not one if he or she does not create an atmosphere that promotes employee engagement. For a good leader to engage his or her employees in such manners that promotes teamwork, organizational growth, and employee satisfaction, such leader evidently must have the ability to relate to employees at their level and then bring them to the level that he or she wants them to be.

This process requires a leader with humility, which

involves self-regulation, self-control, and self-discipline. It is a desire that comes from within. And for humility to rule someone's life, it has to be a thing of the mind, a willing mind for that matter. A willing heart can spark collaboration and relationships.

When a person is willing to take up a challenge, he or she will be humble enough to do whatever it takes to achieve his or her desired goal. Viewing humility from this lens is another way to say that willingness is synonymous with humility.

In their study on humility, Davis and Hook (2014) concluded that humility involves both intrapersonal and interpersonal components. From the intrapersonal perspective, humility involves an accurate view of self. A humble person understands his or her strengths and weaknesses and makes no mistakes to pretend otherwise. Instead, he or she comes to life with wholeness and presence. With this attitude, it makes more sense for a person to be available and attentive to others when he or she is given the opportunity to interact with others.

On the other hand, humility has an interpersonal component when a person allows himself or herself to share space with others in manners that promote relationships. The link that exists between humility and willingness promotes collaboration in any setting (workplace, social, relationship, etc.). So it is fair to suggest that willingness strongly contributes to collaboration.

Safe Environment

At all times, personal safety is a priority in every aspect of life. When a person feels threatened, he or she will likely not pay too much attention to anything but focusing on how to secure his or her safety. In this context, an unsafe environment—whether internal or external—is critical and predicts how one is willing to collaborate.

In a work environment, employees who deem the site as hostile tend to lack the zeal and motivation to go to work on a regular basis. These feelings could be rooted in management attitudes toward employees, lack of proper work equipment, rigid work schedule, and a whole host of other negative factors. Such an environment infects the habit of collaboration. But hope is not lost. Commonsense prescriptive measures are available to help create an environment of collaboration.

For Managers and Leaders of Organizations

- Acknowledge there is a problem. A common mistake that managers and leaders make in organizations is to pretend with employees—to maintain that everything is fine even in the face of obvious confusion. Employees are not stupid individuals. They are human beings who happen to be employees of one company or another. In most cases, an employee is someone's spouse, parent, coach, entrepreneur, and so forth. The worst thing some leaders and managers do is reduce or label their employees and assume they can only perform at that level of responsibility. This misleading assumption undermines the potential of their employees. So managers and leaders should admit that there is a problem and learn how to treat their employees as potential leaders.

- Be willing to have a heart-to-heart conversation with an employee. Managers and leaders should not be stuck on titles or positions, ignoring the enormous intelligence employees can offer in organizational development. Leaders and managers should be humble and willing to collaborate with employees in levels that trigger intellectual conversations. Such exercise promotes healthy work environments and fosters collaboration. Intellectual humility and cultural humility are powerful elements in collaboration. No matter how much one knows, always allow others to exercise their God-given intelligence, and be willing to learn from one another.

- Avoid micromanagement. Collaboration cannot exist in an airtight atmosphere, a surrounding that sucks the life out of everyone who works in such a space. After creating an environment of free information and collaboration, allow employees to be themselves by demonstrating what they have learned from managers and leaders. People are the products of their environments. If you want to measure the success of any organization, talk to their employees because they are a reflection and an extension of their organizations.

FOR EMPLOYEES OF ORGANIZATIONS

- **A boat and a paddle analogy:** Employees and management are like a boat and a person who paddles the boat. While a boat is built well to sail in waters, somebody still has to paddle the ship to a direction of relevance. Human capital is the foundation of every organization; management is the compass by which employees navigate the waters. Therefore, nobody is more important than the other. Instead, one needs the other to sail through the waters of life. Employees should understand that without a person paddling the canoe, the boat is essentially useless. Therefore, employees should allow management to exercise the training and experience they have acquired through leadership schools and practical applications. There is a reason why managers and leaders occupy those positions of authority.

- **Respect to be respected:** Employees should be willing to respect the authorities of their organizations. In return, respect is reciprocated. No human being in his or her right mind would bite the hand that feeds him or her. When employees give respect to their superiors, this exercise eventually has to rub off in the environment, and a dose of respect infects everyone. Even when management is not maintaining its side of the responsibility, be the bigger person, and respect them anyway. In due time—and if exercised long enough—respect is reciprocated. Stay steadfast to doing the right thing even when the environment tempts you to do otherwise.

- **Make every day count:** The optimistic act of working with one another encourages a life of gratitude. When employee and management understand the art of collaboration, living through life, as opposed to struggling through it, becomes easier and more meaningful. As intelligent employees are in any organization, intellectual humility is a virtue. While employees may be more intelligent than their managers are, employees should give management the benefit of the doubt by respecting them anyway, an act of intellectual humility.

Willingness is directly tied to collaboration, which runs in the wheels of willingness. Without the willingness of heart, collaboration would be short lived. Willingness bridges the gap between dreams and reality. Willingness is best exercised in an atmosphere of great awareness and self-regulation and in a safe environment.

References

Bolygo, Z. "Lessons on Winning and Profitability from Jack Welch. https://blog.kissmetrics.com/winning-and-profitability.

Davis, D. E., and J. N. Hook. "Humility, Religion, and Spirituality: An Endpiece." *Journal of Psychology and Theology* 42, no. 1 (2014): 111–117. http://search.proquest.com/docview/1562513092?accountid=35812.

Prime, J., and E. Salib. "The Best Leaders Are Humble Leaders." https://hbr.org/2014/05/the-best-leaders-are-humble-leaders.

Reynolds, G. S., and W. E. K. Lehman. "Levels of Substance Use and Willingness to Use the Employee Assistance Program." *The Journal of Behavioral Health Services & Research* 30, no. 2 (2003): 238–48. http://search.proquest.com/docview/205229304?accountid=35812.

Sapolin, D. "8 Ways You Should Play Hooky from Work." http://www.forbes.com/sites/nextavenue/2014/02/03/8-ways-you-should-play-hooky-from-work.

Van Lange, Paul A. M., C. E. Rusbult, S. M. Drigotas, X. B. Arriaga, B. S. Witcher, and C. L. Cox. "Willingness to Sacrifice in Close Relationships." *Journal of Personality and Social Psychology* 72, no. 6 (1997): 1,373–1,395. doi: http://dx.doi.org/10.1037/0022-3514.72.6.1373.

CHAPTER 4

EMPOWERMENT

Grossing over forty billion dollars, one of the wealthiest men in the world refuses to will his estate to either his children or grandchildren. Instead, he promised to pay their tuitions to attend any university of their choice and to the highest level. He empowers them to take advantage of his wealth and educate their minds and, in return, use the knowledge to build their own empires. Upon graduation, he pledges to give each one a million dollars to start their own establishments. Now it is left to both children and grandchildren to study hard and graduate in order to claim the promises.

Empowerment is one of the most powerful tools any human being can experience. Self-efficacy, as social psychologist Albert Bandura introduced, is very empowering and revealing. For example, earning a degree from an accredited university opens up a litany of opportunities:

- A son is empowered by his father to take a mantle of life and continue his legacy.
- A mother empowers her daughter on how to live the life of a virtuous woman.
- A teacher empowers a student to become the head student in the class.
- The medical board empowers medical doctors to practice medicine.
- A psychological board of examiners empowers psychologists to administer psychological testing.
- An aviation board empowers pilots to operate aircrafts.
- An institute of electrical and electronic engineers empowers engineers to advance technology.

Empowerment is golden as it is a key that unlocks locked doors. Empowerment liberates, sets captives free, and allows one to see windows of opportunities. It gives the hopeless hope and the weak strength. It resurrects dead emotions, it rekindles souls, and it unites.

This chapter explores the possibilities associated with empowerment and the way it connects to collaboration. I will discuss two outstanding African American inventors, Lewis Latimer and Garrett Augustus Morgan, to demonstrate how empowerment is linked to collaboration.

In this context, I present empowerment from a position of self-efficacy (knowing your capabilities), which posits the ability for someone's beliefs on his or her own capabilities to exercise control over his or her own functioning and events that affects his or her life (Bandura 1994).

Self-efficacy is an internal or psychological form of empowerment. Lewis Latimer and Garrett Augustus Morgan invented products still widely used today. But their products gained a global stage through the help of others. Collaboration from that aspect is what this chapter is all about. I will also discuss employee empowerment in how it relates to collaboration from behavioral and psychological scopes.

LEWIS HOWARD LATIMER

Lewis Latimer (1848–1928), an African American, invented a few products that are still in use today. Growing up in an era when opportunities for African Americans to thrive in America were slim, he believed in himself and the enormous possibilities of his talent.

Without going too much into history, the focus of this chapter is to connect empowerment with collaboration. I recommend readers to research these inventors and dig deeper into their contributions to humanity.

A Princeton University website recorded Thomas Edison as the inventor of the electric light bulb. But give more credit to Thomas Edison for causing the glowing bright light to emanate within a room. His invention changed the way people used to live in the dark. But the light bulbs had a short life span (only lasting for two days), compelling Latimer to start looking for a way to make them last longer.

While working at the United States Electric Lighting Co., owned by Hiram Maxim, Latimer evidently devised a way of encasing the filament to make the light last longer, encouraging the use of electric lighting to be installed within homes and throughout the streets (Loassy 2014).

Latimer's contribution to improving the light bulb was a result of working at Maxim's Company, which suggests an act of collaboration. Latimer received a patent for locking racks for hats, coats, and umbrellas, which were used in several public places, including hotels buildings, restaurants, office buildings, and so forth. He invented other products after then.

Latimer's journey into inventing products was sparked by his discovery of the enormous power of self-efficacy (self-empowerment) and collaboration with others. Several other inventors have proven that self-efficacy and collaboration work hand in hand, including Garrett Augustus Morgan.

GARRETT AUGUSTUS MORGAN

Garrett Morgan (1877–1963), an African American, invented and patented the traffic signal, which he later sold to General Electric. He invented the traffic lights we enjoy today. Even though Morgan only had a sixth-grade education, he believed in himself, which positioned him to thrive. He realized that he was good with his hands, which means he was mechanically inclined. Self-discovery can catapult one into a place of relevance.

Morgan's major breakthrough was his invention of the safety hood, also called a gas mask, gear that firefighters wear to fight fire. It prevents burns and allows air to circulate while in the line of duty.

Considering the racially charged era when Morgan invented the gas mask, he had to fight against social justice to gain recognition in the South. As an African American man, he had a difficult time selling the gas masks to fire departments in the South. He decided to hire an actor friend to pose as an inventor while he dressed up as an Indian chief. The actor would then announce that Big Chief Mason would go inside a smoke-filled tent for ten minutes. When Morgan emerged after twenty-five minutes unharmed, people were amazed. Business boomed. As a determined fellow, he collaborated with his friend, who helped him achieve his goal, to market his product (gas mask) in the South.

Life is designed in such a way that, if you run up against Mountain, you have to decide what to do. Either you go around the mountain, drill holes, or climb to get to the top. Bottom line, you must get to the mountaintop. That shows an attitude of empowerment.

Latimer and Morgan understood the power of empowerment and collaboration. Their tenacity to reach their achieved goals is a testimony to that effect. They understood the importance of living their dreams (to live a life of impact). Their stories should be a source of strength and demonstrate the extent that human spirit could go for recognition. If others ignore recognition, it diminishes quality of life, especially as humans. We coexist and like to be praised.

Coexistence is the essence of collaboration in all facets of life, be it a social setting, relationship, or workplace. The workplace is where people spend a majority of their time. Morgan and Latimer had their breakthroughs in the workplace. So if the workplace has such an impact on working together, a significant amount of time should be focused on how to make the workplace more empowering and collaborative.

EMPLOYEE EMPOWERMENT

Studies show that empowerment is behavioral and psychological, and the effect of employee empowerment supports the notion that there are two folds to empowerment. Let's focus on employee empowerment as it relates to job satisfaction. This means that employee empowerment was measured from a job satisfaction perspective and behavioral aspect as well. Research concluded that the positive aspects related to job satisfaction are related to the colleagues and physical conditions (Pelit, Ozturk, and Arslanturk 2011).

The way employees relate to each other and their environment has everything to do with how empowering and satisfied they feel. From an organizational psychology point of view, management should pay attention to those two factors (the way they relate to each other and the work environment). If these factors are in place, employees feel empowered. Conversely, if employees are unable to relate to each other in a positive view, then they might feel disconnected or disengaged.

In this context, collaboration in the workplace is linked to employee empowerment. That is, employees who feel that their opinions are valued and matter in their organization are likely to collaborate in their environment to ensure that their contributions bring organizational growth and promote organizational commitment. While this is an achievable quest, how can employees and management tap into this idea of empowering one another?

HOW CAN AN EMPLOYEE TAP INTO SELF-EFFICACY?

- **"Knowledge rightly applied is power"**: It is critical to acquire knowledge in any field of training. We can acquire this knowledge through education or experience, for example, attending trade school or a higher institution. In this approach of acquiring knowledge, an individual is expected to attend classes and do a certain amount of coursework for a specific amount of years before graduating from that academic training. Upon completion, a certificate or diploma is conferred, showing completion of the program. On the other hand, empowering by experience suggests that an individual volunteers his or her time through organizations (profit or nonprofit) to gain knowledge. Several organizations allow such. Some are food banks, cancer societies, and United Nations outreach efforts. This kind of experience is common among people who are willing to learn from experienced people in the field. Malcolm Gladwell popularized the rule that it takes ten thousand hours of dedicated practice to master a specific task (Gallo 2014). While this is not the focus of this chapter, it is worth noting that repetition of one particular exercise or work leads to routine and perfection. This thought applies to life at large. That is, when employees realize that the more they work on projects long enough, the more they master such projects. And in the process of mastering a project, it builds confidence and empowerment. Therefore, employees should understand this exercise and cling to it. To feel empowered in the workplace comes with experience and knowledge.

- **Exercise intellectual humility:** It is good to be a think tank in a particular field, but it's greater to be humble about it. An employee should master his or her project very well, but it's critical that the employee understand the importance of intellectual humility. It simply suggests that intelligent minds are still expected to be humble. Therefore, employees should not be arrogant or pompous because of their intelligence in one particular area of training. Instead, they should come to their knowing with a measure of humility.

HOW CAN MANAGERS EXERCISE SELF-EFFICACY TO THEIR EMPLOYEES?

- **Managers should recognize their employees' good deeds:** It is important for managers to regularly celebrate their employees. Celebration in this context is not suggesting that managers throw a block party every day for their employees. Instead, recognize the person the moment that he or she does something beyond his or her call of duty. When employees are appreciated, it encourages them to do more for themselves and the company. So managers should harness the idea of recognizing employees every opportunity they get.

- **Be honest and fair:** Managers should genuinely recognize their employees without any bias or favoritism. Most employees can sense unfairness and phoniness from their managers. Such feelings affect the work environment and employee morale. Managers should avoid faking recognition to their employees because it counteracts the very essence of employee acknowledgment. Appreciations as simple as shaking an employee's hand for a job well done to buying gift cards to a football game in town should have the same effect as offering a day paid off for a job well done. To promote employee empowerment, managers should avoid unfairness and phoniness. Instead, they should be practical and involving.

In this chapter, we learned the enormous presence of empowerment as it relates to collaboration. We learned how African American inventors, Lewis Latimer and Garrett Morgan, empowered themselves by believing in themselves, which made them able to interact with others to invent products (gas masks and a filament that makes light bulbs last longer) that are widely used across the globe to save lives and light up the world.

Empowerment in the context as it was discussed in this chapter relates to self-empowerment. It can also educate us on how management can learn from it to create an atmosphere that fosters employee empowerment. Evidently, whenever an individual feels empowered, whether in the workplace or any other setting, collaboration becomes the vehicle that keeps human relationships growing in a healthy way.

Collaboration cannot exist without an act of words and deeds. One cannot claim collaboration without exchange of knowledge, either virtually or physical. In this context, communication is the vehicle to which collaboration exists.

The next chapter will speak on the subject of

effective communication, one aspect of collaboration that requires skills and engagement. For a person to be able to collaborate strategically, he or she will need effective communication. I will also explore how communication is a critical element in collaboration, which will be difficult to achieve when messaging is distorted. When a project is ambiguous, it creates role conflict whereby nobody knows what to do and when to do it. In this process, communication and collaboration are punctured.

References

Bandura, A. "Self-Efficacy: Albert Bandura, Stanford University." http://www.uky.edu/~eushe2/Bandura/BanEncy.html.

Gallo, Carmine. "Forbes: The Shortcut to the 10,000 Hour Rule." http://www.forbes.com/sites/carminegallo/2014/06/28/the-shortcut-to-the-10000-hour-rule.

IEEE. "IEEE Global History Network: Lewis Latimer Biography." http://www.ieeeghn.org/wiki/index.php/Lewis_Latimer.

Pelit, E., Y. Öztürk, and Y. Arslantürk. "The Effects of Employee Empowerment on Employee Job Satisfaction." *International Journal of Contemporary Hospitality Management* 23, no. 6 (2011): 784–802. doi: http://dx.doi.org/10.1108/09596111111153475.

PBS. "Garrett Augustus Morgan." http://www.pbs.org/wgbh/theymadeamerica/whomade/morgan_hi.html.

Loessy, J. "Celebrating Black History Month - Lewis Latimer." http://www.princeton.edu/africanamericanstudies/news/archive/index.xml?id=9513.

CHAPTER 5

EFFECTIVE
COMMUNICATION

The essence of communication is to be heard and understood, which must be in play for communication to be effective and functional. That is, if one is missing in the process, then messaging is distorted, thereby becoming miscommunication or misunderstanding. Each time there is a miss in communication, interaction, or any kind of exchange of ideas, it indicates a messaging malfunction. By implication, we should take communication, whether verbal or nonverbal, seriously because it determines the next course of action in any setting. For example,

- Marriage discords erupt when there is deficiency in spousal dialogue.
- An average student does poorly in class and exams chiefly due to lack of understanding about the subject, instructor, or both.

- A friendship breaks up for the sheer fact of misunderstanding, which originates from an erosion of communication.
- A troubled teenager leaves home to room with his troubled friends due to lack of dialogue with his parents, caretakers, or guardians.
- A teenage daughter runs off from her parents with an unwanted pregnancy, seeking validation elsewhere due to family dysfunctions.
- Employee morale and job satisfaction is punctured when management withholds employee praise and recognitions.

The list is endless what a misguided communication can cause in human relationships.

In 2013, an Association for Talent Development publication reported Bob Nelson's article that showed 60 percent of employees hardly receive praising from their managers. This means that 60 percent of employees are hardly appreciated by their managers. The article suggested six ways to communicate effective praising:

- Praise the employee as soon as the achievement is complete or the desired behavior is displayed.
- Be sincere about the praising by not using it as a manipulative tactic.
- Be specific when praising an employee.
- Be personal about it by meeting employees face-to-face when possible.

- Be positive about it and avoid using the word *but* at the end of praising.
- Be proactive by praising employees more frequently.

The US Department of Health attributes 70 percent of work-related physical and mental complaints to stress (Garms 2013). It is critical to communicate these stats to readers to educate them, in hopes that such information will better equip leaders to understand the danger of stress in the workplace and the importance of employee praise in the workplace. Managers are as good as their employees.

That is, employee dynamics reflect the leadership of the organization. No employee can rise higher than the leadership of the company, meaning that organizational leadership is as strong and effective as its employees are.

A publication on Association of Talent Development journal posits that the quality of communication within a team of employees or providers affects job satisfaction, retention rate, and patient satisfaction and safety (Becker 2015). This seems to suggest that effective communication improves collaboration. To test this assumption and to find out how strong or weak an organization is, check with the human resources department records for employee turnover rate, employee complaints, the number of employees in the EAP, workplace incivility report, critical incident report, and so forth. This information will prove the health status of the organization. And all these issues could be rooted in a communication gap between employees and management.

A study shared in *Consulting Psychology Journal* discussed the differences in individualistic Western culture (e.g., United Kingdom and United States) and collectivist Asian culture (e.g., China, Singapore, Vietnam, and Malaysia) on a team project in a Hong Kong graduate-level class. When the Western culture instructor asked the team to pick which of the topics of choice would be discussed, after a complete silence for a minute or so, one of the team members said, "Okay, we've decided that we will talk about …"

The Western instructor was surprised because no actual dialogue was conducted. Instead, they used nonverbal language to make a decision based on the spokesperson's prior working experiences with the team. He understood the looks that the other team members gave to each other.

And on that basis, he made a judgment about which was the most appropriate topic (Freedman et al. 2012). Obviously, it was appropriate in a collectivist culture, whereas each team member in an individualistic culture would be expected to contribute as a person and not as a group.

I share this experience to suggest how powerful communication is, especially in a multicultural environment. Evidently, what could be deemed normal in Western culture could be viewed as abnormal in others. For this reason, it is critical to pay attention to nonverbal communication because it could support or interfere with the verbal messages that a person is delivering (Preston 2005). But as long as the dynamics are observed and understood, communication has taken place, and collaboration is in play.

Understanding these dynamics and others encourages effective communication in every setting (workplace, social, relationship, etc.). Communication in these contexts is mutual and progressive. It creates room for inclusion and acceptance. Let us as practitioners and citizens exercise this approach of communication by accommodating one another and understanding as Tracy Kantrowitz cited in *The Industrial-Organizational Psychologist Journal*, "It's often said that the only constant in life is change."

One of the ways to entertain life challenges is to be flexible and approachable. Mastering effective communication and a mind-set of inclusion could create a new way of viewing messaging. To foster this exercise of effective communication, certain behaviors fuel negative atmosphere or feelings, and those experiences poison human relationships, particularly in the workplace.

EXAMPLES OF POOR COMMUNICATION SKILLS

Communication can be deemed poor when the intended message was not conveyed. That is, when the messenger lacks a constructive way of articulating his or her intentions and expresses himself or herself negatively or in such a way that poses discomfort or pain to the receiver, communication breakdown has occurred.

We will now attempt to explore only the two most common ways that communication can be poorly received, particularly in the workplace.

MICROAGGRESSIVE BEHAVIORS

Microaggressive behavior is a suppressed emotion expressed negatively, which usually happens when a person exhibits gestures that offend the receiver. In some cases, the aggressor has done it so many times that it becomes a memorized emotion. Microaggressive behavior indicates an unexpressed subliminal message. The questions to ask in this instance should bring about such behavior and ways it could be addressed. These simple but powerful questions could help control aggressive behavior and violence in the workplace.

Examples of microaggressive behaviors are talking over someone during conversations, avoiding eye contact during conversation, ignoring a person in a hallway or office elevator, and so forth. Although these examples may seem pedestrian, they speak volumes in the life of the receiver.

If not properly addressed, these could escalate into violence over time and become *internalized oppression*, also considered a self-destructive behavior where a person turns hateful behaviors and thoughts toward himself or herself. So we should pay attention to those microaggressive behaviors because they could become a complex condition over time.

PLAYING THE BLAME GAME

Some managers are fond of blaming employees when a project goes wrong. The moment that blame is assigned to a person without proper investigation, communication breakdown has occurred. While people make occasional mistakes, dwelling on mistakes dwarfs relationships and collaboration.

A good manager should find out why a breakdown happened in a project. What could have been done differently? How could this be avoided in the near future?

Shifting energy from blaming to collaborating or investigating will strategically focus attention on the solution, as opposed to the problem or blame. Therefore, a simple advice to leaders and individuals in general is to avoid the blame game because it is a poor means of communication. Learn how to address an issue without attacking the personality of people involved.

In this chapter, we discussed statistical evidence that shows that 60 percent of employees are underpraised by their managers and 70 percent of work-related mental and physical complaints are rooted in stress. We discussed six ways to increase a dose of employee praise. I gave some pointers to avoid poor communication skills.

This chapter marks the end of the five principles of collaboration. I hope that the briefness of each chapter draws readers' attention to the critical elements that will help all of us develop healthy relationships through collaboration.

The next two chapters will attempt to establish the importance of consistency and punctuality. The chapters were purposefully designed to remain present and diligent while exercising these five principles. The idea is to incorporate these two elements as a measurement tool to stay on track throughout this journey called life.

REFERENCES

Becker, E. "Training That Is Vitalizing Communication in Healthcare." *Association for Talent Management* (February 2015).

Freedman, A. M., C. S. Ng, C. Hill, and J. Warrier. "Consulting in International Contexts: Examining and Testing Assumptions." *Consulting Psychology Journal: Practice and Research* 64, no. 4 (February 2015): 252–253.

Garms, E. T. "Practicing Mindful Leadership." *Training + Development* (February 2015).

Kantrowitz, T. "Change Is Constant in I-O Psychology Practice." *The Industrial-Organizational Psychologists* 50, no. 2 (February 2015): 77.

Nelson, B. "A Dose of Positive Reinforcement Can Go a Long Way." *Training + Development* (February 6, 2015).

Preston, P. "Nonverbal Communication: Do You Really Say What You Mean? *Journal of Healthcare Management* 50, no. 2 (2005): 83–6. http://search.proquest.com/docview/206728725?accountid=35812.

Ralston, M. "Upstream in the Mainstream: Strategies for Women's Organizing." *Canadian Woman Studies* 20, no. 3 (2000): 176–180. http://search.proquest.com/docview/217461499?accountid=35812.

CHAPTER 6

DILIGENCE

At beautiful Waikiki Beach in Hawaii, Andy, a ninety-five-year-old violinist, has been entertaining visitors from all over the world for over forty years. Andy plays all sorts of songs from gospel to classic. At age ninety-five, Andy still comes to life with exuberance and vigor. His old, rugged violin still produces the melody of ages, bringing tears of joy and pleasantness to passersby. Andy's attitude toward life stirs up emotions of gratitude and hopefulness. His approach to life attracted an eighty-seven-year-old grandma and widow to flirt with him in anticipation of companionship. It was like a love scene at Waikiki Beach.

The perfect picture of romance and grace, as Andy has painted, raises questions to young minds at the beach. If Andy still comes at life with such energy and passion at his age, what could possibly be our excuse for not living life to the fullest? Without further wasting time, I approached Andy to find out how one could retain such an optimism and grace toward life.

Andy, in a calm but whispering voice, said to me, "Life at Waikiki."

He further explained that his trip to Waikiki Beach every Saturday had made him a better person because each time he came to the beach, he looked forward to playing to his fans as if it were his last entertainment.

I said to myself, *People should come to life like Andy does.*

Andy's story is ours. It depicts each and every one of our lives. We come to life with a mind-set that age is not on our side, our days are behind us, and not in front of us, or we can have the attitude of gratitude like Andy does. Diligence is one quality that humbles the meek at heart. It separates winners from quitters and motivates the humble to believe that "after rain comes shine." Diligence pushes us to keep living in hopes that life is a stage. We either get on stage and perform our best or sit on the sidelines and watch others get on their platforms. The choice is ours, "To be or not to be." In the journey of life, diligence is a compass with which to navigate through life. Let's use a traveler analogy to demonstrate diligence.

A traveler is driving to a destination, a place promised to have all he wished. He convinced and prepared himself for the journey. Studying the road, he learnt that the roads are bumpy and unpaved, and, in some cases, there are detours, but it definitely leads to his desired destination.

On his way, a police officer stopped him and cited him for traveling too slow. He has twenty-one days to report to court or pay the fine. The court administrative office is five miles out of his way. On the seventh day, he decided to drive to the courthouse to pay the fine. He retraced his way and continued his journey. There were thunderstorms, rain, and hail. He contemplated returning to his starting point, but his commitment to reach his final destination got in the way.

If he stays on track, he will surely and eventually make it to his final destination. Diligence keeps you moving when every force suggests otherwise. Diligence is found in what Dr. Daniel Goleman called *productive cocoon*, a place where distractions are filtered, blocked, and avoided. Diligence detests distraction and disorganization. It dwells in a productive cocoon.

Let us apply diligence on each of the five principles to see how they all connect to collaboration.

TRUST

Diligence keeps us trusting in ourselves even when situations suggest otherwise. If we stop trusting ourselves, nobody will have confidence in us or *for* us. The fact that we cannot run away from ourselves is the mere reason why we should trust ourselves so others can have faith in us in due time. In other words, it is appropriate not to trust oneself. At the same time, recognize that nobody can trust you more than yourself.

So to interact with other elements in life, one has to diligently give himself or herself permission to be distrusted and then trusted again. These are the complexities of life. And when we come to life as whole, then we can share completeness with others. So by applying trust as a mechanism for collaboration, we allow ourselves to diligently improve and grow in a healthy atmosphere.

RESPECT

Respect is a conscious exercise that is done in an atmosphere of mutuality and understanding. And for respect to exist, diligence is required. Diligence suggests that, even though some people do not deserve to be respected, do so anyway for the sake of harmony and coexistence.

Interestingly, diligence allows a person to take charge of his or her own decision making and for careful assessment of response and seeing the big picture. Diligence deals with whole and not part. It allows a person to see the complete picture from the beginning.

For example, a student who wants to graduate must study diligently, take required exams, and complete all the necessary requirements as the institution presents. When all measures are taken, the end result is almost always conclusive. When all these factors (respect, diligence, and collaboration) are in place, life is viewed as a whole.

WILLINGNESS

The willingness to collaborate in any setting (workplace, social, relationship, and so forth) requires diligence (consistency). Diligence encourages focus, repetition, and a clear goal. So for willingness to endure the test of time, diligence has to be present. It separates doers from dreamers. Doers apply action to their dreams, while dreamers lack action. So the willingness to diligently apply thoughts into action translates into collaboration.

Alan Percy, the head of counseling at the University of Oxford, noted that doctoral students in arts, social sciences, and humanities have a more isolated and less structured experience in pursuing their degree than science students. His study suggested that these students "have to be far more self-regulated and motivated, but also more resilient to the inevitable disappointments and confusion of exploring what can feel like overwhelming area of research."

With such pressure facing doctoral students in these fields, diligence has to be one construct that will sustain them through the tough time of obvious psychological stress associated with pursuing a doctorate degree.

EMPOWERMENT

Diligence is energy-intensive. It directs and establishes parameters. When diligence is in force, empowerment is activated. For example, a student does not necessarily graduate because of his or her intelligence. Instead, diligence is at work. Intelligence would get a student started, but diligence would keep him or her on track until graduation.

Self-empowerment can be a vehicle that diligence operates on. That is, the will to meaning empowers an individual to do the impossible. And to continue improving and developing, diligence is required.

COMMUNICATION

To become an effective communicator, training and diligence is required. According to a recent study from the University of Bistro, suppressing automated thought and tapping into our creativity is easier to do when we collaborate with others (Castellano 2015). Collaboration is evidently a powerful ingredient for creativity, particularly when working in a team.

Working in a team requires communicating with one another, and diligence is at the forefront to produce tangible results through communication and collaboration. A constant exchange of ideas cannot establish long-lasting results or impressions without the act of diligence.

For its worth, diligence is the wheel that sustains collaboration at a higher level. Effective communication is a continuous exercise that requires diligence. And for collaboration to be well established, diligence needs to be incorporated.

In this chapter, we have learned the importance

of diligence in collaborating with others. We utilized Andy's analogy to demonstrate how diligence can have a long-lasting effect on what we do as individuals. We have also discussed how each of the principles connects to diligence.

The essence of this chapter is to emphasize the importance of paying attention to diligence because it is the driving force to achieve lifetime goals, whether to become a person of integrity, a good spouse, parent, manager, student, janitor, waitress, or into whatever spectrum life launches us. Diligence makes an impression last for a lifetime. On the contrary, it can also be misdirected by committing atrocities. So use diligence as an agent of positive change.

Chapter 7, the final chapter of this book, discusses time management. People obviously feel that there is not enough time to do all they want to do in a day. But interestingly, a study explains otherwise. In the context of which this book is based on, time is a critical element in collaboration. It determines how, what, where, and when things are done. In other words, time even suggests our moods. So if we understand how crucial time is in human relationships, maybe we can be a bit cautious with it. Or maybe we learn to maximize it on a daily basis.

As we dive into the chapter, I suggest that you take a mental flight on how diligent or negligent you have been with your time. What can you do differently to better utilize your hours, minutes, and seconds? And of course, appreciate the gift of time.

REFERENCE

Percy, A. "Studying a PhD: Don't Suffer in Silence." http://www.theguardian.com/higher-education-network/blog/2014/mar/25/studying-phd-dont-suffer-in-silence-seek-support.

Castellano, S. "Neuroscience 'No Brainers' for Trainers." *Training + Development* (February 2015).

CHAPTER 7

TIME MANAGEMENT

William Penn's famous quote, "Time is what we want most, but what we use worst" (Shankar 2015), puts in graphic terms how reckless and careless we are with time. People oftentimes misuse their time in doing something of less importance than what is essential. I would like to take a conventional approach in addressing this topic.

First, it would be reasonable to discuss how time has been a pivotal part of life. Second, we came to life through a process that a time line measured.

THOUGHT PROCESS

Most people came into this world through natural birth. (Some came through artificial insemination, test tube, and so forth.) Based on the assumption of natural mating, time brought two people together in the name of courting. Through dating, they decided to get married (under normal circumstances). They spent some time planning the wedding and eventually got married. After wedding comes intimacy and, ultimately, pregnancy. Time harnesses the baby into a full term of pregnancy. At the due date, the baby was delivered. With time, the baby started to learn how to recognize colors, faces, the scent and sound of the mother, and mother's touch.

With time, the baby started to learn how to sit up, crawl, stand, walk, and, ultimately, run. A few months later, he or she was taken to daycare and, after several years, to Montessori, progressing on to eventually attain his or her highest academic accomplishment. Time secures a graduate his or her first job and more positions to come. Eventually, time would allow the same graduate to become a contributing citizen of the community. Time presents a suitor for relationship and ultimately marriage. Then children come along, and the life cycle completes its course. Time brings a person to old age and eventually the grave.

Notice that the life journey is a bundle of time travel and adventures. The question remains: if time is what we need the most, why are we being reckless with it? From relationship perspectives, spouses spend more time criticizing each other as opposed to complimenting one another. Friends spend more time gossiping and slandering one another than building each other up. Organizations are busy finding ways to increase productivity and performance, thereby neglecting employee-management relationships and well-beings.

The point of this analogy is to suggest that spending time backbiting one another does not necessarily build strong relationships. Instead, it brings confusion and division between parties involved along the process. And when the process of healthy relationship is abused, the individual's well-being is affected.

I will next highlight five areas that individuals find most important to their well-being and how, when these five factors are not well established, it can result in the individual's out-of-balance experience. Therefore, organizations need valuable time to ensure that individuals in their organizations are adequately taken care of.

WORKPLACE IMPLICATIONS

The Association for Talent Development journal shared a critical study conducted by Tom Rath and Jim Harter, concluding that high well-being employees lead to lower health costs and turnover rate. Well-being, as Tom Rath and Jim Harter presented, refers to how well people are balanced in these five areas:

- **Career:** enjoying how they spend their time each day
- **Social:** experiencing strong relationships
- **Financial:** having the ability to manage finances effectively to reduce stress and increase security
- **Physical:** having good health and enough time to get things done on a daily basis
- **Community:** engaging in community activities

The same study also noted that those employees with "thriving" well-being had 41 percent lower health-related costs compared to "struggling" employees, a difference of $2,993 per person (Brotherton 2012). Roth and Harter's study concluded that employees with high-quality friendships at work are seven times as likely to be engaged in their work. From financial perspectives, employees who manage finances well or have financial security have three times the effect of income alone on employees' overall well-being. And finally, employees with high physical well-being have more energy, deal with stress better, and get more done faster.

Employees involved in their communities promote their organization's image and make a positive impact in their lives as well (Brotherton 2012). If organizational leaders can make time to study the importance of employee well-being and apply recommendations prescribed by researchers, organizational leaders will be better and more productive.

Time management is a huge subject in the business world. However, more needs to be done to balance employee-management relationships as it relates to organizational well-being. By implications, organizational and employee well-being are critical in overall community and the nation's well-being.

FUTURE STUDY

Not enough studies have been done on to what extent organizational/employee well-being affects overall national well-being. It would be an interesting study to examine to determine how such a study could influence national waste on health care, psychological health of individuals, and economic health of a country.

As several research studies have shown, physical and mental complaints in the workplace are rooted in stress (Garms 2013; Clay 2011; Korki 2012; Martin 2012). It would be reasonable to look at how stress in the workplace, relationship, social, and school combine to shape national well-being.

While future studies need to be conducted to measure time spent in researching the overall well-being of a nation from organizational, psychological, and economical perspectives on stress, it is reasonable to pay attention to how much time individuals spend on spirituality and psychological well-being. For example, how much time does an average person spend in being alone, exercising meditation, performing yoga, or participating in any spiritual-related activities? Not only will taking personal responsibility on issues of spiritual intelligence using the five principles of collaboration, as shared in this book, encourage quality time, it will also incite self-efficacy, self-inventory, and spiritual awakening in building human relationships. Mindful leadership is another approach necessary to take in improving personal and professional effectiveness of overall organizational productivity (Garms 2013).

The principles shared in this book are attainable. To observe these principles, it is practical to value time management, which means to increase consciousness on how we manage our hours. It is also necessary to measure how and where we spent time and who we spent it with.

By creating awareness on how important time management is, people will start to realize that they have more available, specifically more than they could imagine. Our biggest challenge is how we allocate our time on something of no merits.

I present a simple draft of time analysis to demonstrate how we generally spend time on a daily basis. Some people might work more hours than others do, while some might sleep more than others and so forth. Hopefully, you would be able to trace where you spend your most time and how you can improve your time management.

PRACTICE TIME MANAGEMENT

- We have twenty-four hours a day and seven days a week.
- 24 hours/day x 7 days/week = 168 hours
- Work: 8 hours/day x 5 days = 40 hours
- Sleep: 8 hours/day x 7 days = 56 hours
- Work + Sleep = 96 hours
- 168 hours/week - 96 hours = 72 hours

How do we manage seventy-two hours in a week?

DISCUSSIONS

There are certain truths about the concept of time. At the same time, there are certain myths about time concept as well. Finally, we look at the implications of time.

THE TRUTH ABOUT TIME

- **We all have twenty-four hours in a day.** Every one of us comes into any day expecting to have twenty-four hours' worth of experience. No one gets an additional hour or fewer. In other words, great minds that we have either read, heard, and know about have the same twenty-four hours in a day. The only difference was how they managed their time. If you were asked to give an account of your day, what would be your response: excuses, denial, and blame or grateful, eventful, productive, and so forth? Only you can answer these questions because, in the topography of your mind, you get to decide what kind of day you would like to have. In truth, every human being under the sun experiences twenty-four hours in a day, and nobody has more or less.

- **We all have seven days in a week.** In a week, we experience a total of 168 hours. Every one of us experiences the same amount of hours every week. Whether we live in Timbuktu or the hinterland, we all have the same number of hours in a week. The question remains how we spend that week. We can argue that we worked forty hours in a week based on an eight-hour workday. We can also assert that we slept fifty-six hours in a week based on eight-hours per day worth of sleep. Based on these claims, we have only spent ninety-six hours between work and sleep in a week's period. This means that we still have seventy-two hours (three days) in a week unaccounted for. Statistically, we can literarily say that we had a weekly dose worth of sleep and work and still have an excess of seventy-two hours (three days) unaccounted for. Based on these stats, what did you do with that seventy-two hours worth of time in a week? Take pen and paper, and write down your activities for the day in details. After writing down your activities, ask yourself what was important, essential, and worthless or useless. After your analysis, decide what area is essential to you, and allocate more time developing your essentials and your importance. You will be amazed how your life will change after practicing it for twenty-one to thirty days.

- **No given day repeats itself.** This is a fact of life. We can never experience any day twice. Instead, we can create that day as a memory in the theater of our minds but never repeat the exact same day. Now, having known that no day repeats itself, it would be a gift to make the best out of every given day without holding grudges or regrets. Treat every second as the last one because no day repeats itself. Don't be part of those groups who live in an illusion about time, thereby procrastinating their lives away.

THE MYTHS ABOUT TIME

- **We can make up lost time.** Once time is lost, it is gone forever. Time wasted can never be regained. Make every effort to seize the moment because the next minute is not guaranteed. There is a true story about a man who was living in a foreign land and only visited his parents once every two years. As a medical student at a prestigious university and ambitious to sit for his medical exams, he received a message from his relatives that his father was seriously sick. Now he was faced with a dilemma: to skip his exams and travel to visit his father in a foreign land or to sit for his medical exams and visit his father after finishing his exams. Having struggled with his dilemma, he decided to transfer funds for his father's medical bills and other expenses and to visit after the exams. He took the tests. He was preparing to travel to visit his father when he received another message that his father had passed. In grief and pain for the loss, he attended his father's funeral. Upon arrival to his home base, he received a letter from his university notifying him that he did not pass his medical exams. It was the shock of his life. He forfeited visiting his father so he might sit for his medical exams. Incidentally, he failed his tests and never met his father alive again. In his situation, he thought in his mind that he could make up the lost time with his father as soon as he finished his exams. Unfortunately, he lost his father, never to regain his lost time with him, and ultimately failed his tests. The lesson to be learned in this story is that there is no such thing as making up lost time.

- **We can gain time by working faster.** A military slogan states, "Slow is smooth, and smooth is fast." This means that, if you are bouncing around, you can't really see what's happening around you. In other words, take time to do it right the first time. When things are done under immense pressure without thorough planning, they usually end up being done haphazardly. Therefore, there is no such thing as regaining lost time. Do it right the first time because there is never going to be another time like the lost time. We can either utilize our time judiciously or be reckless with it. The choice is ours.

THE IMPLICATIONS OF TIME

- **Time waits for nobody.** It is ever-changing. Even as I'm writing this text, time is constantly ticking. It waits for nobody. If there is such a thing as stopping time, most people would stop their biological clock so they could stay young forever. But because nobody has a monopoly over time, it waits for nobody. With time, all we have is the ability to make the best out of it.

- **Time is a precious gift.** While we are alive, we should make the best out of time. Each hour we have with our loved ones should be cherished because it is a gift. Make good use of it.

- **Time has a "chameleon effect."** Research shows that the chameleon effect refers to the tendency to adopt the postures, gestures, and mannerisms of interaction partners (Lakin et al. 2003). If we can borrow this language, we can conclude that time does whatever we want it to do for us. That is, if we want time to work in our favor by utilizing our time judiciously, then it will work in our favor. But if we are reckless with time, then it will be our worst enemy (so to speak). So we can make time work for or against us. The choice is ours. Make good use of time to educate, motivate, inspire, and volunteer for just causes. Those are the most productive and rewarding ways to make good use of time.

REFERENCES

Black Hawk Down. "Orientation: Cast Members Learn the Ropes." http://www.military.com/ContentFiles/BHD moviePR.

Brotherton, P. "High Well-Being Leads to Lower Health Costs and Turnover Rates." *Training + Development* (February 2015).

Clay, R. A. "Is Stress Getting to You?" *Monitor on Psychology* 42, no. 1 (February 2011): 59.

Garms, E. T. "Practicing Mindful Leadership." *Training + Development* (February 2015).

Korkki, P. "Workstation Building a Bridge to a Lonely Colleague." Accessed February 8, 2015. http://www.nytimes.com/2012/01/29/jobs/building-a-bridge-to-a-lonely-colleague-workstation.html.

Lakin, J. L., V. E. Jefferis, C. M. Cheng, and T. L. Chartrand. "The Chameleon Effect as Social Glue: Evidence for the Evolutionary Significance of Nonconscious Mimicry." *Journal of Nonverbal Behavior* 27, no. 3 (2003): 145–162. http://search.proquest.com/docview/229313827?accountid=35812.

Martin, S. "Virtual Therapy: Our Health at Risk." *Monitor on Psychology* 43, no. 3 (February 2015): 18.

Shankar, S. "Time Management Quotes." https://www.academia.edu/3810355/Time_Management_Quotes.

CLOSING THOUGHTS

Studies and analogies presented in this book demonstrate that each construct in these five principles plays a critical role in collaboration. In other words:

1. Trusting oneself has a fundamental influence on how to trust another person. It is difficult to trust others when one does not have confidence in himself or herself. So trusting oneself is the first step to having a healthy trust relationship with another person. Also, understanding there is more than one type of trust (e.g., goodwill, contractual, and competent) helps determine what level of trust to share with an individual, as opposed to discrediting a person based on an overarching type of trust. When people relate to each other via the lens of different types of trust, they can develop healthy relationships. And when a healthy relationship is established, people are one step closer to having a collaborative experience.

2. Respect enhances collaboration. When people feel respected, they tend to experience healthy associations, whether in the workplace, social sphere, or relationship. So collaboration is profound in an environment of respect.

3. Willingness refers to willpower. When a person behaves in certain ways that demonstrates engagement and commitment, an act of willingness is experienced. And when willingness is present, collaboration is promoted.

4. Empowerment is one aspect of collaboration that encourages a person to be himself or herself. A sense of empowerment compels an individual to go above and beyond the call of duty. Empowerment empowers employees to experience a sense of belongingness and meaningfulness. And when a sense of belongingness and meaningfulness are present, performance and productivity improves.

5. Communication is a pivotal part in a collaborative effort. Effective messaging brings clarity and focus. When information is transmitted in such a manner that stirs up a positive response, effective communication has taken place. And when effective communication is present in a conversation or interaction, it encourages

collaboration. So the essence of communication is to be understood.

Diligence and time management are critical elements in human existence. To be known for something requires repetition and consistency. And these two constructs combined equals diligence.

Character is built out of diligence. The act of doing something particular repeatedly, especially for a good cause, highlights diligence, which sustains passion, which then sparks interest.

But diligence sustains passion. Even when passion fades away, diligence remains throughout the struggle. Time management intertwines with diligence because being disciplined in something requires doing the same thing repeatedly until it's mastered. And mastering anything requires dedicating time and energy in grasping such a thing. So observing the importance of time in any aspect of life is the key to withstand challenges of life, knowing that life is a collection of memories remembered with events, space, and time.

It is noble to note that for human relationships to improve, there must be a collaborative effort to all parties, irrespective of social status, gender, age, religion, class, and so forth. What affects one directly impacts all indirectly. And when human relationships are in harmony, other elements will enjoy the peacefulness and tranquility such peaceful collaboration brings.

I hope this book provides sufficient data that would encourage readers to seek deeper understanding on how to relate to one another without building imaginary walls as defense mechanisms. Live life as if you only have sixty seconds to live.

INDEX

ABOUT THE AUTHOR

J. Ibeh Agbanyim earned his graduate degree in industrial-organizational psychology, and he is pursuing his doctoral degree in industrial-organizational psychology at Grand Canyon University. He is a distinguished award recipient from the department of psychology for his exemplary leadership and significant contribution to academic excellence at the University of Ibadan. He is a graduate affiliate of Association for Talent Development, International Leadership Association, Informing Science Institute, Society for Consulting Psychology, and many others.

Agbanyim is the founder of Focused Vision Consulting, LLC, and has been a senior logistics associate at UPS for the past eighteen years. He is the author of two books, *The Power of Engagement* and *Fear*. He has been a presenter and guest speaker for different organizations and institutions, including the University of Ibadan, Nigeria; First Bank of Nigeria Insurance; and American Society for Quality in Orlando, Florida. He has been an invited guest at the Napoleon Hill Think and Grow Rich Stickability Tour in Toronto, Canada, and the International Convention for Psychological Science in Amsterdam, the Netherlands.

He can be reached at powerofengagement@att.net and www.fvgrowth.com.

Made in the USA
San Bernardino, CA
06 April 2016